EMMANUEL JOSEPH

Harmonies of the Human Brain, The Intersection of Music, Neuroscience, and Anthropology

Contents

1

Chapter 1: The Origin of Music

Music, as an art form, has a profound history that traces back to the dawn of human civilization. From the rhythmic beating of stones and sticks to the melodic chants of ancient tribes, music has always been an intrinsic part of human culture. It is a universal language that transcends geographical boundaries and cultural barriers, binding people together in a shared experience of sound and emotion. The origin of music is deeply rooted in the need for communication and expression, serving as a medium to convey stories, emotions, and cultural heritage.

Anthropologists have found evidence of early musical instruments, such as flutes made from bird bones, dating back to around 40,000 years ago. These findings suggest that music was not only a form of entertainment but also played a crucial role in the social and spiritual lives of early humans. Music was used in rituals, ceremonies, and communal gatherings, creating a sense of unity and belonging among members of a community. The rhythmic patterns and melodic structures of these early musical forms were influenced by the natural sounds of the environment, such as the chirping of birds and the rustling of leaves.

As human societies evolved, so did the complexity and diversity of their musical expressions. Different cultures developed unique musical traditions, instruments, and styles, reflecting their distinct histories and values. For example, the ancient Greeks believed that music had the power to influence human behavior and emotions, a concept known as the "Doctrine of Ethos." This belief was reflected in their musical practices, which were closely associated with religious rituals, theater, and education. Similarly, in many African cultures, music is intertwined with dance, storytelling, and oral traditions, serving as a vital means of preserving and transmitting cultural knowledge.

The study of the origin of music also reveals fascinating insights into the cognitive and neurological aspects of musical perception and production. Researchers have discovered that musical abilities are deeply embedded in the human brain, with specific neural pathways and regions dedicated to processing musical information. This suggests that the capacity for music is an innate human trait, shaped by both biological and cultural evolution. Understanding the origin of music, therefore, not only sheds light on the development of human culture but also offers valuable insights into the fundamental nature of human cognition and creativity.

2

Chapter 2: The Neuroscience of Music

The relationship between music and the human brain is a captivating area of study that has garnered significant attention from neuroscientists. Music engages a complex network of brain regions, including those involved in auditory processing, motor control, emotion, and memory. When we listen to music, our brains rapidly analyze the incoming sound waves, breaking them down into their constituent elements, such as pitch, rhythm, and timbre. This intricate process is facilitated by the auditory cortex, which plays a central role in decoding and interpreting musical information.

One of the most intriguing aspects of the neuroscience of music is its ability to evoke powerful emotional responses. Research has shown that listening to music can activate the brain's reward system, releasing neurotransmitters like dopamine that contribute to feelings of pleasure and euphoria. This explains why certain songs can elicit strong emotional reactions, such as chills or goosebumps. The limbic system, which is responsible for regulating emotions, also plays a crucial role in our emotional response to music. Music can evoke a wide range of emotions, from joy and excitement to sadness and nostalgia, depending on factors such as tempo, harmony, and lyrical content.

Another fascinating area of research is the impact of music on brain plasticity, or the brain's ability to adapt and reorganize itself. Studies have shown that musical training can lead to structural and functional changes in the brain, particularly in regions associated with auditory processing, motor skills, and memory. For instance, musicians often exhibit enhanced connectivity between the left and right hemispheres of the brain, as well as increased gray matter volume in areas related to auditory perception and motor coordination. These findings suggest that engaging with music can have profound effects on brain development and cognitive abilities.

Moreover, music has been found to have therapeutic applications in various clinical settings. Music therapy, which involves the use of music to address physical, emotional, and cognitive needs, has been shown to be effective in treating conditions such as depression, anxiety, and neurodegenerative disorders. The therapeutic benefits of music are attributed to its ability to modulate brain activity, reduce stress, and promote relaxation. Additionally, music can serve as a powerful tool for social bonding and communication, particularly in individuals with autism spectrum disorders or other communication challenges. Overall, the neuroscience of music highlights the intricate connections between musical experience and brain function, revealing the profound impact of music on human cognition and well-being.

3

Chapter 3: The Anthropology of Music

Anthropology, the study of human societies and cultures, offers valuable insights into the role of music in human life. Music is not only a form of artistic expression but also a social phenomenon that reflects the values, beliefs, and traditions of different cultures. Anthropologists study music as a cultural artifact, examining how it is created, performed, and consumed within various social contexts. This approach sheds light on the diverse ways in which music influences and is influenced by cultural practices and social dynamics.

One of the key areas of interest in the anthropology of music is the concept of musical identity. Music often serves as a marker of individual and collective identity, allowing people to express their sense of self and belonging. For example, traditional folk songs and dances are often associated with specific ethnic or regional groups, embodying their unique cultural heritage. Similarly, contemporary music genres, such as hip-hop or rock, can serve as symbols of subcultural identity, providing a sense of community and solidarity among fans. Anthropologists explore how musical practices contribute to the construction and negotiation of identity, both at the personal and societal levels.

Another important aspect of the anthropology of music is the study of musical rituals and ceremonies. In many cultures, music plays a central role in religious and ceremonial practices, serving as a means of communication with the divine or the supernatural. For instance, in West African religious traditions, drumming and chanting are integral components of spiritual rituals, believed to invoke the presence of ancestral spirits or deities. Similarly, in Native American cultures, music is used in healing ceremonies and rites of passage, facilitating a connection between the physical and spiritual realms. By examining these practices, anthropologists gain a deeper understanding of the symbolic and functional roles of music in different cultural contexts.

The anthropology of music also explores the impact of globalization and technological advancements on musical traditions. As cultures interact and exchange ideas, musical practices are often influenced and transformed by external forces. For example, the spread of Western popular music has led to the hybridization of musical styles, resulting in new genres that blend traditional and contemporary elements. Additionally, the advent of digital technology has revolutionized the production and distribution of music, enabling artists to reach global audiences and collaborate across geographical boundaries. Anthropologists study these phenomena to understand how music evolves and adapts in response to changing social and technological landscapes.

4

Chapter 4: The Emotional Power of Music

Music has a unique ability to evoke and amplify emotions, making it an essential part of the human experience. From the jubilant rhythms of a celebration to the melancholic melodies of a farewell, music has the power to capture and convey the full spectrum of human emotions. This emotional resonance is one of the reasons why music is such a powerful and enduring art form, capable of touching the hearts and souls of people across different cultures and generations.

The emotional power of music can be attributed to several factors, including its structural elements, such as melody, harmony, and rhythm. For example, a slow, minor-key melody with descending patterns may evoke feelings of sadness or longing, while an upbeat, major-key tune with syncopated rhythms can create a sense of joy and excitement. The use of dynamics, tempo changes, and timbre variations also contributes to the emotional impact of music, allowing composers and performers to create nuanced and expressive musical experiences.

In addition to its structural elements, music's emotional power is deeply connected to its ability to trigger memories and associations. Hearing a particular song can transport us back to a specific moment in our lives, evoking vivid recollections of people, places, and events. This phenomenon, known as music-evoked autobiographical memory, highlights the strong link between music and memory. The brain's limbic system, which is involved in both emotion and memory processing, plays a crucial role in this process. By tapping into our personal and collective memories, music can evoke a wide range of emotions, from nostalgia and sentimentality to exhilaration and empowerment.

The social and cultural context in which music is experienced also influences its emotional impact. Music often serves as a medium for expressing and sharing emotions within a community, creating a sense of connection and solidarity. For example, national anthems and protest songs can evoke feelings of patriotism and unity, while love songs and ballads can resonate with our innermost feelings of affection and longing. In many cultures, music is an integral part of communal gatherings, such as weddings, funerals, and festivals, providing a shared emotional experience that strengthens social bonds.

Furthermore, music's emotional power can have therapeutic effects on our mental and emotional well-being. Listening to or creating music can serve as a form of emotional expression and regulation, helping us process and cope with difficult emotions. Music therapy, which involves the use of music to address emotional and psychological needs, has been shown to be effective in treating conditions such as depression, anxiety, and post-traumatic stress disorder. By providing a safe and creative outlet for emotional expression, music can promote healing and resilience, enhancing our overall quality of life.

5

Chapter 5: The Cognitive Benefits of Music

The cognitive benefits of music extend beyond its emotional impact, offering valuable insights into the complex interplay between music and the human brain. Research has shown that engaging with music, whether through listening, playing, or composing, can enhance various cognitive functions, including memory, attention, and problem-solving skills. These benefits are not limited to musicians; even casual listeners can experience cognitive improvements through regular exposure to music.

One of the most well-documented cognitive benefits of music is its positive effect on memory. Studies have demonstrated that music can enhance both short-term and long-term memory, making it easier to recall information. This phenomenon, known as the "Mozart Effect," suggests that listening to classical music can temporarily boost spatial-temporal reasoning abilities, which are essential for tasks such as mathematics and engineering. Additionally, music has been found to improve verbal memory and linguistic skills, particularly in children who receive musical training. These findings highlight the potential of music as a powerful tool for cognitive development and learning.

Music also plays a crucial role in enhancing attention and concentration. The structured and repetitive nature of music can help train the brain to focus on specific tasks, improving attention span and reducing distractions. For instance, background music with a steady rhythm and moderate tempo can create an optimal environment for studying or working, helping individuals maintain focus and productivity. Furthermore, music's ability to evoke emotions can enhance motivation and engagement, making it easier to stay concentrated on a given task.

Problem-solving and creative thinking are other cognitive domains that can benefit from musical engagement. Music encourages divergent thinking, which involves generating multiple solutions to a problem and thinking outside the box. This creative process is facilitated by the brain's ability to make connections between different neural pathways, a skill that is honed through musical improvisation and composition. Musicians, in particular, often exhibit enhanced problem-solving abilities, as they must navigate complex musical structures and adapt to changing musical contexts in real-time.

In addition to its direct cognitive benefits, music can also promote overall brain health and resilience. Regular engagement with music has been shown to reduce the risk of cognitive decline and neurodegenerative disorders, such as Alzheimer's disease. This protective effect is attributed to music's ability to stimulate neural activity, promote brain plasticity, and reduce stress. By fostering a healthy and active brain, music can contribute to overall cognitive well-being and longevity.

6

Chapter 6: The Social Functions of Music

Music is a powerful social tool that brings people together, fostering connections and creating a sense of community. Throughout history, music has played a central role in various social functions, from celebrations and rituals to protests and political movements. By examining the social functions of music, we gain a deeper understanding of how it shapes and is shaped by human interactions and social structures.

One of the primary social functions of music is its ability to facilitate communication and expression. Music provides a universal language that transcends verbal barriers, allowing individuals to convey emotions, ideas, and stories. For example, folk songs and ballads often serve as vehicles for storytelling, preserving oral traditions and historical narratives. In many cultures, music is an integral part of religious and spiritual practices, serving as a means of communication with the divine or the supernatural. By offering a shared medium for expression, music enables individuals to connect on a deeper emotional and spiritual level.

Music also plays a crucial role in social bonding and cohesion. Communal musical activities, such as singing, dancing, and drumming, create a sense of unity and belonging among participants. These activities often occur during important social events, such as weddings, festivals, and religious ceremonies, reinforcing social ties and cultural identity. In many African cultures, for instance, music and dance are inseparable from social life, serving as a means of bringing communities together and fostering a sense of collective identity. The shared experience of making and enjoying music strengthens social bonds and promotes a sense of solidarity.

In addition to its role in social bonding, music can also serve as a powerful tool for social change and activism. Throughout history, music has been used to challenge social norms, raise awareness, and inspire collective action. Protest songs and anthems, for example, have been central to various political and social movements, from the civil rights movement in the United States to anti-apartheid struggles in South Africa. These songs often convey powerful messages of resistance and hope, galvanizing individuals to unite and advocate for social justice. By giving voice to marginalized communities and promoting social consciousness, music can drive positive social change.

Moreover, music can serve as a means of cultural exchange and understanding. In an increasingly globalized world, musical collaborations and cross-cultural influences have become more prevalent, fostering mutual appreciation and respect among different cultures. Music festivals and events, such as the World Music Festival, bring together artists and audiences from diverse backgrounds, celebrating the richness and diversity of global musical traditions. By facilitating cultural dialogue and exchange, music promotes empathy and understanding, contributing to a more inclusive and interconnected world.

7

Chapter 7: The Impact of Music on Mental Health

The impact of music on mental health is a topic of growing interest, as researchers and clinicians explore the therapeutic potential of music for various psychological conditions. Music has been found to have a profound effect on mental health, offering a range of benefits, from reducing stress and anxiety to enhancing mood and emotional well-being. The use of music therapy, in particular, has gained recognition as an effective treatment modality for various mental health issues.

One of the primary ways in which music positively impacts mental health is through its ability to reduce stress and promote relaxation. Listening to calming music, such as classical or ambient music, can activate the parasympathetic nervous system, which is responsible for the body's rest and relaxation response. This can lead to a reduction in heart rate, blood pressure, and cortisol levels, helping individuals feel more relaxed and at ease. Additionally, engaging in musical activities, such as playing an instrument or singing, can serve as a form of mindfulness, allowing individuals to focus on the present moment and alleviate stress.

Music has also been shown to be effective in alleviating symptoms of anxiety and depression. The emotional resonance of music can provide a sense of comfort and solace, helping individuals cope with difficult emotions.

For example, listening to music that resonates with one's emotional state can provide a sense of validation and understanding, reducing feelings of isolation and loneliness. Music therapy, which involves the use of music interventions to address emotional and psychological needs, has been shown to be particularly effective in treating depression and anxiety. By providing a safe and creative outlet for emotional expression, music therapy can enhance emotional well-being and resilience.

In addition to its calming effects, music can also enhance mood and promote positive emotions. Upbeat and energizing music, such as pop or dance music, can boost mood and increase feelings of happiness and motivation. The rhythmic and melodic elements of music can stimulate the release of endorphins and dopamine, which are associated with pleasure and reward. This explains why listening to our favorite songs can evoke feelings of joy and excitement, enhancing our overall mood and well-being.

Furthermore, music can serve as a powerful tool for social connection and support, which are essential for mental health. Group musical activities, such as choirs, bands, and drum circles, provide opportunities for social interaction and bonding, reducing feelings of social isolation. Music can also facilitate communication and expression, helping individuals articulate their thoughts and emotions in a supportive environment. By fostering a sense of community and connection, music can contribute to improved mental health and overall quality of life.

8

Chapter 8: The Role of Music in Childhood Development

The role of music in childhood development is a topic of significant interest, as researchers and educators recognize the numerous benefits that musical engagement can offer to young children. From enhancing cognitive and motor skills to fostering social and emotional development, music plays a crucial role in supporting the overall growth and well-being of children. Incorporating music into early childhood education can provide a rich and stimulating environment that promotes learning and development.

One of the key benefits of music in childhood development is its positive impact on cognitive abilities. Research has shown that musical activities can enhance various cognitive functions, including memory, attention, and problem-solving skills. For example, learning to play a musical instrument requires the ability to read music, coordinate movements, and memorize patterns, all of which contribute to improved cognitive abilities. Additionally, exposure to music has been found to enhance language development and literacy skills. Singing songs and nursery rhymes, for instance, can help children develop phonemic awareness, vocabulary, and comprehension.

Music also plays a crucial role in motor development, as it involves the coordination of fine and gross motor skills. Playing musical instruments, such as drums or keyboards, requires precise hand-eye coordination and finger dexterity, helping children develop their motor skills. Dancing and movement activities set to music can also promote physical development, as they encourage children to use their bodies in various ways, improving balance, coordination, and spatial awareness. These physical activities not only support motor development but also contribute to overall health and well-being.

In addition to its cognitive and motor benefits, music has a profound impact on social and emotional development. Group musical activities, such as singing in a choir or playing in an ensemble, provide opportunities for social interaction and collaboration. These activities teach children important social skills, such as teamwork, communication, and empathy. Music can also serve as a means of emotional expression, allowing children to explore and articulate their feelings. For example, playing or listening to music can provide a safe and creative outlet for emotions, helping children develop emotional intelligence and resilience.

Furthermore, music has the potential to create a positive and engaging learning environment that fosters creativity and imagination. Musical activities often involve elements of play and improvisation, encouraging children to think creatively and explore new possibilities. This creative process not only enhances cognitive and emotional development but also promotes a love of learning and self-expression. By incorporating music into early childhood education, educators can create a dynamic and enriching environment that supports the holistic development of children.

9

Chapter 9: The Cultural Significance of Music

The cultural significance of music is evident in its ability to convey and preserve cultural values, traditions, and identities. Music serves as a repository of cultural knowledge, capturing the essence of a society's beliefs, customs, and history. Through its melodies, rhythms, and lyrics, music reflects the unique cultural heritage of different communities, providing a rich tapestry of human experience.

One of the ways in which music embodies cultural significance is through its role in rituals and ceremonies. In many cultures, music is an integral part of religious and spiritual practices, serving as a means of communication with the divine and a way to mark important life events. For example, traditional chants and hymns are often sung during religious services, creating a sense of reverence and connection to the sacred. Similarly, music is used in various rites of passage, such as weddings, funerals, and initiations, to symbolize transitions and celebrate milestones. These musical rituals not only reinforce cultural values but also strengthen social bonds within the community.

Music also plays a crucial role in preserving and transmitting oral traditions. In societies where written language may not be prevalent, music serves as a powerful medium for storytelling and the dissemination of cultural knowledge. Folk songs, ballads, and epic tales are often passed down through generations, preserving the history, legends, and wisdom of a community. For instance, in many African cultures, griots are traditional musicians and storytellers who play a vital role in maintaining the oral history of their people. By singing and playing instruments, griots keep alive the cultural narratives and heritage of their communities, ensuring that these stories are not lost to time.

Furthermore, music is a reflection of cultural identity and diversity. Different musical genres, styles, and instruments are often associated with specific cultural groups, serving as markers of identity and pride. For example, the vibrant rhythms of samba and bossa nova are emblematic of Brazilian culture, while the intricate melodies of classical Indian music reflect the rich heritage of India. Music can also highlight the diversity within a culture, showcasing the various regional, ethnic, and linguistic traditions that coexist. By celebrating this diversity, music promotes a sense of cultural appreciation and mutual respect.

In an increasingly interconnected world, the cultural significance of music extends beyond individual societies to encompass global cultural exchange. Music acts as a bridge between cultures, facilitating cross-cultural understanding and collaboration. Through musical fusion and innovation, artists from different backgrounds come together to create new and exciting sounds, enriching the global musical landscape. For instance, the fusion of traditional African rhythms with contemporary Western genres has given rise to unique musical styles such as Afrobeat and world music. This cultural exchange not only enhances the creativity and diversity of music but also fosters a greater sense of global unity and interconnectedness.

10

Chapter 10: Music and Language

The relationship between music and language is a fascinating area of study that sheds light on the cognitive and neural mechanisms underlying both forms of communication. Music and language share several similarities, including their use of sound, rhythm, and structure to convey meaning. Understanding the interplay between music and language can provide valuable insights into human cognition, communication, and cultural development.

One of the key similarities between music and language is their reliance on sound and rhythm. Both music and language use variations in pitch, tempo, and intensity to convey information and emotions. For example, the rising intonation in a question and the descending intonation in a statement are analogous to the melodic contours in a musical phrase. Similarly, the rhythmic patterns in speech, such as syllable stress and timing, parallel the rhythmic structures in music. These auditory and rhythmic elements engage similar neural pathways in the brain, suggesting a shared cognitive basis for processing music and language.

Another important aspect of the relationship between music and language is their use of syntax and structure. Just as language has grammatical rules that govern the arrangement of words into sentences, music has compositional rules that guide the organization of notes into phrases and melodies. These structural principles allow both music and language to create complex and meaningful expressions. Research has shown that the brain regions involved in processing linguistic syntax, such as Broca's area, are also activated during the processing of musical syntax. This overlap highlights the cognitive connections between musical and linguistic abilities.

The study of music and language also reveals intriguing insights into the development of these skills in early childhood. Infants are born with an innate sensitivity to musical and linguistic sounds, which plays a crucial role in their cognitive and social development. Research has shown that exposure to music and language during the early years can enhance auditory discrimination, memory, and language acquisition. For example, singing lullabies and nursery rhymes to infants can promote their phonemic awareness, vocabulary, and emotional bonding. Similarly, musical activities, such as clapping and dancing, can support the development of motor coordination and social interaction.

Moreover, the relationship between music and language extends to their potential therapeutic applications. Music therapy and speech therapy often intersect, as music can facilitate language development and communication in individuals with speech and language disorders. For instance, melodic intonation therapy (MIT) is a therapeutic approach that uses melodic and rhythmic elements to improve speech production in individuals with aphasia, a condition that impairs language abilities. By tapping into the shared neural pathways of music and language, therapeutic interventions can harness the power of music to enhance linguistic skills and communication.

11

Chapter 11: The Future of Music and Technology

The future of music is being shaped by rapid advancements in technology, which are transforming the ways in which music is created, distributed, and experienced. From digital production tools to streaming platforms and virtual reality experiences, technology is revolutionizing the musical landscape and offering new possibilities for artists and audiences alike. Exploring the intersection of music and technology reveals exciting trends and innovations that are poised to redefine the future of music.

One of the most significant technological advancements in music is the development of digital production tools and software. These tools have democratized the process of music creation, allowing artists to produce high-quality music from the comfort of their own homes. Digital audio workstations (DAWs), virtual instruments, and plug-ins provide musicians with a vast array of sounds and effects, enabling them to experiment and innovate with ease. Additionally, artificial intelligence and machine learning are being integrated into music production, offering new ways to compose, arrange, and mix music. For example, AI-powered algorithms can analyze musical patterns and generate new compositions, assisting artists in the creative process.

The rise of streaming platforms has also transformed the distribution and consumption of music. Services such as Spotify, Apple Music, and YouTube provide listeners with instant access to a vast library of songs from around the world, breaking down geographical barriers and promoting musical diversity. These platforms use advanced algorithms to recommend personalized playlists and discover new artists, enhancing the listening experience. For artists, streaming platforms offer new opportunities for exposure and revenue, allowing them to reach global audiences without the need for traditional record labels. However, the digitalization of music distribution also raises important questions about artist compensation, copyright, and the sustainability of the music industry.

Virtual reality (VR) and augmented reality (AR) are emerging technologies that are poised to revolutionize the way we experience music. VR and AR create immersive and interactive environments that transport listeners to virtual concert halls, festivals, and music videos. These technologies enable users to engage with music in novel ways, such as exploring 3D soundscapes, interacting with virtual performers, and attending live concerts from the comfort of their homes. For artists, VR and AR offer new creative possibilities for storytelling and audience engagement, blurring the lines between reality and imagination.

Furthermore, the future of music is likely to be shaped by advancements in wearable technology and biometric sensors. These devices can monitor physiological responses to music, such as heart rate, skin conductance, and brain activity, providing insights into the emotional and cognitive effects of music. This data can be used to create personalized music experiences that adapt to the listener's mood and preferences. For example, wearable devices can generate real-time playlists that match the user's emotional state or provide biofeedback for therapeutic purposes. By integrating technology with human biology, the future of music holds the potential for deeply personalized and transformative experiences.

12

Chapter 12: Music as a Universal Language

Music is often described as a universal language, a form of communication that transcends linguistic and cultural barriers. Despite the diversity of musical traditions around the world, music has the power to evoke emotions, convey meanings, and create connections among people from different backgrounds. Exploring the concept of music as a universal language reveals its unique ability to bridge divides and foster a sense of shared humanity.

One of the reasons why music is considered a universal language is its emotional resonance. Music has the ability to evoke a wide range of emotions, from joy and excitement to sadness and longing, regardless of the listener's cultural or linguistic background. The expressive power of music lies in its ability to tap into the universal human experience, capturing the nuances of emotion and feeling. For example, a melancholic melody can evoke feelings of sorrow and nostalgia, while a lively rhythm can inspire a sense of celebration and vitality. This emotional universality allows music to communicate in a way that transcends words.

The universality of music is also evident in its ability to convey meaning and stories. Music often incorporates elements such as melody, harmony, and rhythm to create narratives and convey messages. For instance, folk songs and ballads tell stories of love, loss, and heroism, capturing the collective memory and cultural heritage of a community. Even instrumental music, without the use of words, can convey complex ideas and evoke vivid imagery. The ability of music to communicate meaning through sound enables it to serve as a bridge between different cultures and generations.

Furthermore, music's role in fostering social connections and community is a testament to its universality. Throughout history, music has brought people together in various social contexts, from communal rituals and celebrations to protests and political movements. The shared experience of making and enjoying music creates a sense of belonging and solidarity, reinforcing social bonds and cultural identity. For example, national anthems and protest songs serve as powerful symbols of unity.

13

Chapter 13: Music and Human Evolution

The connection between music and human evolution is a compelling area of research that explores how musical abilities may have evolved alongside other cognitive and social traits. Scholars believe that music played a significant role in the development of early human societies, contributing to survival, social cohesion, and cognitive development. By examining the evolutionary origins of music, we gain insights into its fundamental importance to the human experience.

One of the leading theories about the evolution of music is that it served as a form of social bonding and communication. Early humans lived in small, cooperative groups where strong social ties were essential for survival. Music, with its rhythmic and melodic elements, provided a means of coordinating group activities, such as hunting, gathering, and communal rituals. Singing and drumming could have been used to synchronize movements and actions, enhancing group cohesion and cooperation. This social function of music may have been particularly important in fostering trust and solidarity within early human communities.

Another evolutionary perspective suggests that music may have played a role in mate selection and reproductive success. Similar to the elaborate songs and displays of many animal species, early humans may have used music to attract mates and demonstrate their fitness. Musical abilities, such as singing and playing instruments, could have signaled desirable traits such as creativity, intelligence, and social status. This theory is supported by the fact that musical talent and appreciation are often associated with positive social and cognitive attributes. By enhancing reproductive success, musical abilities may have been naturally selected and passed down through generations.

The cognitive benefits of music may also have contributed to its evolutionary significance. Engaging with music requires a range of cognitive skills, including auditory perception, memory, attention, and motor coordination. These skills are essential for various survival-related tasks, such as language acquisition, tool use, and spatial navigation. By promoting cognitive development, musical activities could have provided an adaptive advantage to early humans. Additionally, the emotional and stress-reducing effects of music may have supported mental and physical well-being, further enhancing survival and reproductive success.

Overall, the evolutionary perspective on music highlights its integral role in the development of human societies and cognitive abilities. Music is not merely a cultural artifact but a fundamental aspect of the human experience that has shaped and been shaped by our evolutionary history. Understanding the origins of music in human evolution provides valuable insights into the universal and enduring nature of musical expression.

14

Chapter 14: Music and Healing

The therapeutic power of music has been recognized for centuries, with various cultures using music to promote healing and well-being. Today, the field of music therapy continues to explore and expand the ways in which music can be used to address physical, emotional, and cognitive health. By examining the role of music in healing, we gain a deeper appreciation of its potential to enhance quality of life and support overall health.

One of the primary ways in which music promotes healing is through its ability to reduce stress and anxiety. Listening to calming music can activate the parasympathetic nervous system, leading to a state of relaxation and reduced physiological arousal. This can help lower heart rate, blood pressure, and cortisol levels, promoting a sense of calm and well-being. Music therapy interventions, such as guided imagery and music, use specific musical elements to evoke relaxation and reduce stress, making them effective tools for managing anxiety and promoting mental health.

Music also plays a significant role in pain management. Research has shown that listening to music can reduce the perception of pain and improve pain tolerance. The analgesic effects of music are attributed to its ability to distract the mind, modulate emotional responses, and stimulate the release of endorphins, which are natural pain relievers. In clinical settings, music therapy is used to alleviate pain and discomfort in patients undergoing medical procedures, surgery, and chronic pain conditions. By providing a non-pharmacological approach to pain management, music therapy offers a safe and effective complement to traditional treatments.

The cognitive and emotional benefits of music make it a valuable tool for neurorehabilitation. Music therapy has been shown to improve cognitive functions, such as memory, attention, and executive functioning, in individuals with neurological conditions, such as stroke, traumatic brain injury, and dementia. For example, rhythmic auditory stimulation (RAS) is a music therapy technique that uses rhythmic cues to improve gait and motor coordination in individuals with Parkinson's disease and other movement disorders. Additionally, music therapy can enhance emotional expression and communication in individuals with autism spectrum disorder, providing a means of connecting and interacting with others.

Furthermore, music's social and cultural dimensions contribute to its healing potential. Group musical activities, such as choir singing, drumming circles, and community music-making, provide opportunities for social interaction, support, and connection. These activities can reduce feelings of isolation and loneliness, enhancing social well-being and quality of life. Music therapy sessions often incorporate culturally relevant music, honoring the individual's cultural background and promoting a sense of identity and belonging. By addressing the holistic needs of individuals, music therapy fosters healing on multiple levels, from the physical to the emotional and social.

15

Chapter 15: The Ethics of Music

The ethical considerations of music encompass a wide range of issues, from copyright and intellectual property to cultural appropriation and social responsibility. As music continues to evolve and intersect with various aspects of society, it is essential to examine the ethical implications of musical practices and address the challenges that arise. By exploring the ethics of music, we gain a deeper understanding of the responsibilities and values that shape the musical landscape.

One of the primary ethical concerns in music is the issue of copyright and intellectual property. Copyright laws are designed to protect the rights of creators and ensure that they receive recognition and compensation for their work. However, the digitalization of music and the rise of online sharing platforms have raised complex questions about the enforcement of copyright and the balance between access and protection. Unauthorized copying and distribution of music, commonly known as piracy, can undermine the livelihoods of artists and creators. Addressing these challenges requires a nuanced approach that respects the rights of creators while promoting fair access to musical content.

Cultural appropriation is another ethical issue that has garnered significant attention in the music industry. Cultural appropriation occurs when individuals or groups from one culture adopt elements of another culture without proper acknowledgment or respect for its significance. In music, this can involve the use of traditional musical styles, instruments, or symbols in ways that strip them of their cultural context and meaning. For example, the commercialization of indigenous music or the uncredited sampling of traditional songs can perpetuate cultural stereotypes and exploit marginalized communities. Ethical musical practices require a commitment to cultural sensitivity, respect, and collaboration, ensuring that the contributions of diverse cultures are honored and valued.

The social responsibility of musicians and the music industry is another important ethical consideration. Musicians have the power to influence public opinion, shape cultural narratives, and inspire social change. With this power comes the responsibility to use their platform for positive and constructive purposes. This includes promoting messages of inclusivity, equality, and justice, as well as addressing issues such as violence, discrimination, and environmental sustainability. The music industry also has a responsibility to create fair and equitable opportunities for artists from diverse backgrounds, ensuring that their voices are heard and represented.

Moreover, the ethical considerations of music extend to the impact of music on mental and physical health. While music has many therapeutic benefits, it can also have negative effects when used irresponsibly. For instance, excessively loud music can lead to hearing loss, and certain lyrical content can promote harmful behaviors or perpetuate negative stereotypes. Musicians, producers, and listeners must be aware of these potential risks and take steps to mitigate them, promoting the safe and responsible use of music.

Harmonies of the Human Brain: The Intersection of Music, Neuro-science, and Anthropology

Book Description:

Harmonies of the Human Brain: The Intersection of Music, Neuroscience, and Anthropology delves into the captivating and multi-faceted relationship between music and the human experience. Spanning fifteen insightful chapters, this book explores how music influences, shapes, and reflects our cognitive processes, emotional states, social interactions, and cultural identities.

From the rhythmic chants of ancient civilizations to the intricate compositions of modern-day music, the book traces the origin and evolution of musical expression. It delves into the neurological underpinnings of music perception and production, highlighting the profound impact music has on our brains and cognitive functions. The book also examines the role of music in social bonding, cultural rituals, and identity formation, providing a comprehensive understanding of its significance in human life.

Readers will discover the therapeutic potential of music, as well as its ability to promote mental health and well-being. The book addresses the ethical considerations surrounding music, including copyright issues and cultural appropriation, and explores the future of music in an increasingly digital and interconnected world.

Through a blend of scientific research, anthropological insights, and personal anecdotes, *Harmonies of the Human Brain* offers a compelling exploration of the deep and intricate connections between music, the mind, and culture. Whether you are a musician, a music lover, or simply curious about the mysteries of the human brain, this book promises to inspire and enlighten you on the harmonies that shape our lives.